.......... NJ 07930

# MARKETING

## GUIDES

**for Small Businesses:**

# LOCAL SEO

Ray L. Perry | Phil Singleton

## Marketing Guides for Small Businesses: Local SEO

Copyright © 2015 by Ray L. Perry and Phil Singleton

All rights reserved. No part of this book may be reproduced or transmitted in any form or by any means without written permission of the author.

Trademark Information: All trademarks, trade names, or logos mentioned or used are the property of their respective owners. Every effort has been made to properly capitalize, punctuate, identify and attribute trademarks and trade names to their respective owners, including the use of ® and TM (TM) wherever possible and practical.

Limit of Liability/Disclaimer of Warranty: While the publisher and authors have used their best efforts in preparing this book, they make no representations or warranties with respect to the accuracy or completeness of the contents of this book and specifically disclaim any implied warranties of merchantability or fitness for a particular purpose. No warranty may be created or extended by sales representatives or written sales materials. The advice and strategies contained herein may not be suitable for your situation. You should consult with a professional where appropriate. Neither the publisher nor the authors shall be liable for any loss of profit or any other commercial damages, including but not limited to special, incidental, consequential, or other damages.

www.ducttapepublishing.com

# FOREWORD

### Thoughts on using this guide

Since you've opened this guide I'm guessing you want to grow your business, get better at marketing or maybe just figure out how to acquire that first customer.

So, first off – congratulations. A commitment to life-long learning is the hallmark of any truly committed entrepreneur.

But make no mistake there is more information available than time to consume it and it's very important that you take in a steady diet of practical information created by those that have been where you're trying to go.

This guide certainly meets that criteria.

I know the authors of this guide personally and have seen their work first-hand. They not only consistently deliver results for their clients; both have been very generous in sharing their knowledge by way of training fellow members of the Duct Tape Marketing Consultant Network. I think this speaks volumes because it allows me to confidently assure you that you are about to read some pretty good stuff.

Ray L. Perry and Phil Singleton are two rock star marketing professionals in the Duct Tape Marketing Consultant Network. As certified marketing consultants they:
- Have completed my intensive training program;
- Participate in ongoing marketing training and mentoring;
- Have exclusive access to an arsenal of proven tools and methodologies;

- Are members of an elite, fast-growing global network of talented small business marketing consultants;
- Are certified to install the Duct Tape Marketing System.

At Duct Tape Marketing, we teach that strategy before tactics is the key to creating a winning, high ROI marketing plan. Getting your strategy right from the get-go is the only way to create a web-centric, inbound marketing platform that will consistently draw ideal customers to your doorstep.

Once you get the right strategy in place, however, tactical execution is the only way to ensure that your marketing plan will produce results.

The *Marketing Guides* series, is broken down into logical eBook chunks, and in a practical, easy-to-read format. Each eBook in this series will give you - the business owner - the education you need to understand and apply an important tactic to your business.

I highly recommend this eBook and the entire *Marketing Guides* series. Read this eBook, apply what you learn and there is no question your business will generate more business and more leads. Period.

**John Jantsch**
Author Of *Duct Tape Marketing*
**www.DuctTapeMarketing.com**

# TABLE OF CONTENTS

# INTRODUCTION

## HOW TO GET YOUR PHONE RINGING AND YOUR DOOR SWINGING, USING LOCAL SEO

Phone ringing… that's a good thing. Door swinging, too. If you're a small business owner that depends on a steady stream of new customers, your attention probably perked right up at the prospect of getting more people into your business.

But when you read *Local SEO*, you probably made 'that' face. You know, the same face people make when someone offers them kale ice cream, turkey bacon, or a root canal.

You're not living under a rock. You've heard of search engine optimization, or SEO. In fact, it would be a safe bet to assume your business gets contacted multiple times each week by some firm somewhere promising to propel your small business website straight to the top of Google.

Now you can learn how to get your local business ranked for, well, local customers. Even when people plan on shopping locally, they still look to Google to find out who is most convenient, who's got the best prices, and whose business is popular with all the other local customers. The problem for a lot of small business owners is that the whole local SEO process seems to be veiled in complication and confusion, putting it perpetually on the back burner if it's on the stove at all. Not you, though! You just grabbed this little eBook and that proves you know you've got to do something different.

**Local SEO IS different... so you'll want to pay attention for a few minutes.**

It's how you put your small business on the map (literally) – and it's the best way to make sure your ideal prospects, the ones who are near enough to become your loyal customers, discover you. It's also one of the most cost-effective ways small businesses can compete with bigger competitors. Yes, *that* competitor – the one gobbling up your market share. The one with a presence in every town and city. The one with the seemingly bottomless pockets who's marketing circles around you.

By now, chances are good that you've got a website (even if it's not one you love). Unfortunately, just having a website is not enough to grow your business.

You've got to make sure that it's showing up where your next customers are looking.

It's time to learn about search engines and your online presence, even if your business is in a rock-solid, brick and mortar building, with no online sales. There are still plenty of ways you can use the Internet to grow your business. For instance, did you know that simply by telling Google some BASIC information (we're talking name, address, and phone number here) you can improve your placement in a Google search?

Your ideal customer may be searching right now for the products and services you sell. This new customer has at least two options – you, and your competitor. There's a lot you can do to distinguish your business from your competitors. That differentiation begins with developing a sound marketing strategy, and part of that strategy involves a plan for optimizing your website to attract local customers. After all, it does you no good to attract potential customers who are hundreds or thousands of miles away. You want the customer who's right around the corner, who's ready to buy, and who's trying to figure out which local company is the best choice for the products and services they need right now.

One of those optimization strategies uses a free tool that Google GIVES you to come up with the words and phrases your customers are using to look for your business online. Once you are armed with this kind knowledge, you'll find out exactly where to use those words on your website to drive your ranking straight to the top of Google.

Prepare to be surprised at just how easy (and yet how oddly tricky) it can be. Some of the ideas may ring a bell in the back of your mind (think local Chamber of Commerce). Others are bound to surprise you. For instance, NAPs for your business are not only legitimate, they're crucial! And you'll see that a citation is now a great thing to get. With just this one little eBook, you'll learn more than you imagine about how you can take the kind of action that causes Google to take notice of your local business.

Keep reading, and you'll learn how to use Local SEO to increase the likelihood that new customers find and choose your business. We'll begin with a basic explanation of Local SEO, then go into a few proven tactics you can use to get started putting your local business in front of the customers you want most.

Here's just a quick preview of what you're about to discover:

- Got a smartphone? So does everyone else you know, so make sure your website looks great on a mobile device without your potential customers needing to pinch and zoom, because they won't! They simply won't take the time. They'll just go to your competitor instead. What you're about to learn will make sure that never happens again.

- Do your customers love you and your business? Learn how you can use that goodwill and great reputation to work for your rankings. Local SEO uses your great reviews to spread the word about your business – but you've got to know how to get those reviews in the first place. Keep reading, and you'll know exactly how to do that.

- How social is your business? Are you sending all the right social signals? Do you post, pin, tweet, update, snap and all things social media? If you aren't socially active yet, should you be?

We know that the learning curve to market your business online is steep, but we've taken the basics and put them together here so you can skip a few steps, kind of like using the elevator instead of walking up the stairs. In fact, you might just find out that once you see that there are clear steps you can take, that learning curve will straighten right out.

Many people think that marketing is a necessary evil in business. You might even be one of them. By the time you finish reading this book, you'll understand more about why marketing is necessary, and you might be ready to let go of the thought that it's evil. There are a lot of things about local SEO marketing that really aren't that difficult and once you see your business climbing the search engine rankings, you might even start to enjoy this part of your business. So, go ahead and read on. Your business will never be the same!

# CHAPTER 1

## WHAT IS LOCAL SEO?

Local SEO (Search Engine Optimization) is a procedure for optimizing your website to help it display more prominently in the local search results pages on Google and the other major search engines. Local ranking might not be overly important for large national and international companies like Alcoa Aluminum or Sony Electronics, but if your company has a local address and must draw customers to that address, then an effective local SEO strategy is absolutely vital to the future of your business. To be clear, we are referring to organic search results, as is the non-paid search results. Organic SEO is not to be confused with the pay-per-click advertising, which is always on the right side of the Search Engine Result Pages (SERPs), and most often at the very top of the search result pages. Pay-per-click or PPC ads are marked as ads or sponsored, but typically in small print. Sneaky, huh.

If you're a dentist, plumber, car dealer, auto body shop, or any of hundreds of other kinds of small businesses that depend on a steady flow of local customers calling or walking through the front door, your website must appear at or near the top of local search results.

Let's take a look at how local SEO impacts your business, and how you can take control.

## How Does Local SEO Benefit Your Business?

Local first page search results for most U.S. cities and towns result in at least ten of every kind of local business displayed. That's ten hair salons, ten auto body shops, ten dentists, etc. Sure, some areas have only five, and some have fifty, but on average, most consumers get dozens of local website result choices.

These days, Google and the other search engines are displaying more local results. Yet, they are not only displaying your local competitors, but also competitors from the region and from around the country. In other words, your business is not only competing for ranking spots with local businesses, regional and national companies are vying for those top spots as well. Small local businesses must continue to work hard to get a good spot on the results page.

What's great news is that the search engines can automatically detect the physical location of searchers are when they search, even if they don't specifically type in the name of their city or town. For example, if someone in your geographic area searches for "dentist" without adding a location, the search results will include a list of local dentists. Your website may even be somewhere buried in those results.

What's not such great news is that getting to the top of local results won't just happen automatically. In fact, without a local SEO program it's unlikely you will appear on, or even near, the first page – and if your competitors ARE working on their local SEO, they are more likely to get those new customers instead of you.

## What's at Stake?

If you own and operate a business without a local SEO plan, don't expect to be popping up on the first page of Google for prime keywords. Without taking action, your business will only continue to be lost in the shuffle of back pages. With the increasing trend of localized search results, combined with everyone searching before they buy, your lack of online visibility will eventually lead to a serious business meltdown. Think about it. There are more than **3.5 billion Google searches every day**. Your business growth depends on reaching them when they're searching online because that is where all the action is.

By the time you see your business volume dropping off it could be too late to salvage the situation. This is not high drama. It is reality, and it's already happening to companies right now. If your business has a local address and needs local customers, you must optimize for local search to stay in the game. Simple as that.

If you know how local SEO works you can ask the right questions and then make and execute a plan. Let's take a quick look at the history of SEO and the key elements you should include in your plan.

## A Brief History of SEO

Not long after the creation of the Internet, companies quickly found out that following basic optimization ground rules would increase their chances of getting their websites at or near the top of search results pages whenever a searcher typed in certain words.

Obviously this was a good thing for the companies that followed those ground rules. In fact, the process of using those special optimization rules gave birth to what is now known as Search Engine Optimization – SEO. As SEO became more widely known somebody got the idea that they could make a lot of money by helping companies get better placement in search results. Soon an entire industry sprung up to help companies optimize their websites to get the best search results.

The demand for top search results spots exploded. However, companies quickly discovered one tiny little problem. SEO is a zero sum game. There are only a few spots on the first page of search results. Most people don't bother searching past the first page. In fact, there is a running joke among SEO professionals that the best place to hide a dead body is on the second page of Google. "Googling" has become an integral part of the consumer purchase process and that search behavior has created steep competition for placement on the front page. That's all it took for SEO to become a booming industry.

Before we dive into how you can use Local SEO to grow your business, there's some housekeeping to do on your website. After all, no matter how good of a driver you are, you can't win a race without a fast, high performance car.

# CHAPTER 2

## LOCAL SEO BEGINS AT HOME

$M$uch of what you're about to learn to do to promote your local business online is "out there" – as in not part of your own website. In subsequent chapters, you'll get step-by-step guidance through NAPs, directories, Google My Business, social media, and all that good stuff.

But not yet. Not until you've done what needs doing to your own website. See, Local SEO happens in two places: on-site (on your website) and off-site (everywhere else on the Internet). You may also hear this referred to as on-page SEO and off-page SEO.

Once you've got your on-site situation squared away, it will be a lot easier to handle the off-site tasks. Without proper on-site SEO, your website will never be able to reach its local ranking potential. Once you get it right, your site will actually be working for you instead of just wallowing in the search engine abyss.

The heart of SEO is knowing how to choose and use the right keywords.

## What Is a Keyword?

It is the word or phrase people key into a search engine like Google when they want to search for something. Occasionally, when more than one word is used it is called a key phrase. But whether it's a phrase or a word, it's usually referred to as a keyword. Keywords form the basis for all Search Engine Optimization strategies so before you ramp up your SEO program you must know which keywords your prospective customers are using when searching for your products and services.

## 'Probable-Keyword' Tools & Selecting the Right Keywords

As it turns out, there are some free tools you can use to help develop a list of probable keywords. The most popular is Google's Keyword Planner. This is actually a tool meant for Google's pay-per-click (PPC) service, AdWords. However, it's a great free tool that you can use for SEO keyword research:

**https://adwords.google.com/KeywordPlanner**

Just type in a word or phrase that you think people might use when they search for you. The tool will kick out a list of associated keywords with information about the number of searches done for each keyword per month. It also indicates the competitiveness of each keyword. Meaning how many other companies are engaging in a PPC bidding war for a give word or phrase. This is really useful information, because if the volume, suggested price per click and competition level is high, you know that those keywords correlate to more sales, and thus those are the terms and phrases you should focus on. Proper keyword research takes the guesswork out of SEO.

**Long Tail Keywords**

Naturally, shorter more generic words and phrases have more competition than longer, more specific keywords, called "long-tail" keywords. In general, the more specific a long-tail keyword is, the easier it is for your website to rank when people search for it. As a local business owner you'll be happy to learn that local long tail keywords – like "Plumbing Supplies Atlanta, GA" – appear in over 40% of all Google searches. Meaning if you use the counties, cities, or neighborhoods your company services in your local SEO program, you can radically improve their effect. In other words, you'll want to naturally use various combinations of [city or suburb] + [service] in your web page and blog copy, as well as the other SEO related website code on your site (more on that later).

After you've finished your keyword research you should have scores of potential keywords that might be used by searchers looking for what your company provides. Sounds like a lot, right? Well, it's not. Think about all the possible terms people might use to search for what you do. For example, here's a list of keywords for an Atlanta, GA plumbing company:

Atlanta GA Plumbing Company

Atlanta GA Plumbing Repair

Atlanta GA Plumbing Service
Atlanta GA Commercial Plumbing
Atlanta GA Residential Plumbing
Plumbing Company Atlanta GA
Plumbing Repair Atlanta GA
Plumbing Service Atlanta GA
Commercial Plumbing Atlanta GA
Residential Plumbing Atlanta GA

And that's just the beginning. It's not even counting other terms like toilet repair, septic system, garbage disposal, sump pump, water heater, etc. And of course there are more specific geographic references for areas around Atlanta like Alpharetta, Marietta, Peachtree City, and Athens. Once you start adding in these combinations of variables the list explodes.

Ok, so now you've got a list of a couple of hundred possible keywords. What should you do with them?

### Your Keywords, Your Website

When you look at your website, examine it closely, page by page. Choose one to two keywords per page, and optimize that page for that keyword(s). This includes your Home page.

As you write the content for that page, be sure to include your keyword in a few different places on the page, including:

- **The page title:** this is the browser bar title on your site, and usually the blue clickable title text you see in search engine results.

- **The meta tag** (meta description): This text is not visible on your website, but its typically the text you see under the blue title text within Google search results.
- **The URL structure**
  (i.e. www.yoursite.com/keyword)
- **Image ALT tags and title tags** for any images on your page – Google cannot read graphic text, so you can use computer code to assign a keyword or phrase to every image on your site, so Google knows the context of the image and its relevance to the web page.
- **Anchor links:** Anywhere throughout your text where you include a clickable link to another page on your website (i.e. If you mention one product or service on a page, make a clickable link to that product or service; use your keyword as the clickable anchor text.)
- **Geo-targeted phrases:** Anytime your text includes naturally geo-targeted phrases (like city, neighborhood or suburbs) on a web page or in a blog post.
- **Outbound Global Authority Links:** Whenever you include a clickable link to an authority site in your industry (this is good to do!), providing that it adds value and is relevant to the content on a given page.
- **Outbound Local Authority Links:** Whenever you include a clickable link to a local website (Chamber of Commerce, a local government site, or a local news site), again – providing its natural, relevant and adds editorial value to the page or blog post.

Make sure you don't just stick your keywords anywhere simply to help your SEO efforts. You should only insert them where they fit naturally, add to the content flow, and make editorial sense. As helpful as keywords are to your website, "stuffing" words and links to and from your website can be equally damaging to your website. Google in particular is very good as sniffing out websites that over-optimize or use manipulative SEO techniques to try and game their system. If you stick to quality content that naturally works in keyword phrases into your website, you should not have to worry about search engine penalties. Google has a detailed list of quality guidelines you can find here:

https://support.google.com/webmasters/answer/35769

The anchor text link is a link built directly into the text, rather than a traditional URL link. For example, if the text says "List of our plumbing supplies" and you made that phrase a clickable link, that would be an example of an anchor text link. It is actually quite different and much more common today than telling your website visitors, "For more information on our plumbing supplies visit:

www.atlantaplumbinginc.com/supplies".

You can see how much cleaner the anchor text link is compared to the traditional URL link.

Regarding linking out to other sites, your website visitors might find it helpful if link to other websites that might add some contextual value to that page's content, like to a "Who's Who in Plumbing" website (if you're a plumbing company like the example above). And it's not just to jack up your value with the search engines. Your website visitors will also appreciate it if you have these kinds of links to authoritative resource websites. Simply put, these outbound links improve the overall content of the website, and that's always a good thing.

Next, you'll need to duplicate this procedure for every page on your website. Of course you'll need to do it again whenever you add a new page or a blog post, which you should be doing regularly to enhance your ranking.

## Don't Skimp on Content

It's important to make sure every page on your website has "enough" text to gain the respect of the search engines as a legitimate, valuable page. Part of what determines how a search engine views your pages' value involves how long visitors stay on those pages. If you've got just a little bit of text, they'll read it in seconds and click elsewhere. That's not good.

You want enough words on your pages to say what you need to say, to engage your readers, and to make them stay put for more than ten seconds. Here are some guidelines for content length:
- Home page: 200-300 words
- Core service pages: 300+ words
- Blog posts: 500+ words minimum;

Long form or in-depth blog posts: blog posts of 1,000 to 2,500 words or more are performing better on the search engines these days.

Be sure the text on every page is easy on the eyes. No overwhelming blocks of text. No super-long paragraphs. Use sub-headlines, bullet points, embedded YouTube videos images to make the page appealing.

**Go Mobile!**

The statistics on mobile usage are staggering. Over 50% of all searches are from mobile devices. Odds are good that when your new customers go looking for you online, they're using a smartphone or a tablet. If your website isn't mobile friendly in a mobile responsive design, you're sunk. They'll click to your competitor's mobile responsive site and forget all about you.

There's a saying about mobile: "Pinch and zoom spells your doom." What it means is that if your smartphone-using website visitors can't navigate and use your website (and read what's on it) without having to use their fingers to expand and move your content, you've got a serious problem. In other words: "Thumb-scroll to get the cash to roll!"

When mobile sites first became popular, many companies set up separate websites for desktop and smartphone users. These sites would somehow recognize which kind of machine the user was on, and send them to the appropriate venue. That's old hat now.

Now, the technology is called responsive. It's the same in that it detects whether a visitors is on a desktop or a mobile device, but there is no longer any need for a separate website. Thank goodness, because with two sites, you face double the trouble for optimization tasks!

Not sure whether your website is responsive? Whip out your smartphone and take a look. Can you read and use your site without squinting or doing the old pinch and zoom?

Want a more scientific way to know for sure whether your website is mobile friendly? Just enter your website into this tool, and you'll find out whether Google thinks it is:
https://www.google.com/webmasters/tools/mobile-friendly/

**Introducing The Grand Schema**
Every project has that one phase that's just awful. If you're painting, it's the wall prep. If you're sewing, it's pinning the pattern. If you're building a paver patio, it's tamping the ground.

If you're optimizing your website, it's Schema. It's pretty much a guarantee that you won't want to do this step – but we'd be doing you no favors by not telling you about it.

Schema markup is basically a way you can make your website easier for search engines to find. It tells search engines what your website means instead of what is says. That's every bit as important as it sounds.

Essentially Schema is a format (AKA whole other foreign, techy language) you apply to the HTML code of your web pages to give the search engines the information they need to identify what your content is about. The Schema microdata is what forms rich snippets of your content, which ends up on the search engine results page. (Yes, we know, it hurts!) A common example would be when you see extra information in search results, such as a product star rating or event listings, etc. Schema is special SEO code that tells Google you would like to them to consider showing this extra information to searchers.

Categorizing your content correctly is critical to the search engines' ability to serve up relevant information when people go searching. Irrelevant content in the search engine results is the surest way to lose users… and that translates to billions of dollars in lost revenue.

So, for you, Schema's a big pain in the neck the likes of which we can't adequately convey. For search engines Schema's a significant hurdle they want to watch you jump, in order to make it easier for them to be confident that when they serve up your site to searchers, the searchers will quickly see that they're in the right place.

Even without stepping into Schema, the entire on-site optimization process is time-consuming, not to mention complicated, especially if you've got a descent sized website. That's why reputable Local SEO agencies find that their clients are eager to hand this set of tasks off to them.

OK, that part is over. We apologize in advance for any Schema-themed nightmares you have tonight. It has to be done, but it sure isn't pleasant.

Next up, we'll zero in on how Local SEO works, and what you need to know if you want to remain competitive in your location. While most business owners have a passing understanding of 'regular' SEO, the local business owners who grasp Local SEO are the ones who get a steady stream of new customers coming in.

# CHAPTER 3

## WHY YOUR BUSINESS NEEDS A NAP

Every industry has its acronyms. For Local SEO, one you're likely to hear a lot is NAP. It stands for Name, Address, and Phone number. NAP plays a surprisingly important role in getting your business listing onto the map of local search results.

These simple bits of information can do wonders for your local marketing efforts if you handle them correctly – and tank you if you don't. It is critically important that the NAP be consistent not only throughout your website, but also anywhere it appears throughout the entire Internet. Why? Because the big search engines use NAP data when figuring out which companies to display in area-targeted searches. If your NAP is inconsistent across the Internet, it will hurt your local SEO efforts.

Here's what's most important as you work on your NAP:

## NAP Accuracy

Search engines use NAP as a way to verify the existence of a company. In order for the search engine to confirm the existence and legitimacy of your company, it is programmed to ensure that every data point aligns exactly.

How bad is it if your NAP is inaccurate? Bad. A mismatched NAP is one of the main negative local ranking issues impacting how a website is ranked. In fact, according to a recent Google study, the number one negative ranking factor is a listing detected at a phony or incorrect business location. The same study said the number three negative factor is a mismatched NAP. Obviously, these kinds of inaccuracies will destroy your local SEO efforts if they're not corrected – and quickly.

## NAP Consistency

Accuracy is one issue, and consistency is another. The NAP information on YP.com must be consistent with Superpages, which must be consistent with Kudzu, and so on throughout the entire Internet. You might be surprised to see how many online business listings are out there for your business that are incorrect – a wrong street number, a misspelling, or even an incorrect phone number. Once you start looking, you'll probably wonder how these incorrect NAP elements got out there, because certainly if you'd created the listing, it would have been correct!

Sometimes the problem originates with a change in your business contact information. It's not always easy to maintain consistency, especially in today's fast changing business environment. For example, you may decide to move, or get an 800 number, or make a small change to the company name. So how do you ensure that all your NAP listings are consistent? You can either hire somebody or do it yourself. Most small business owners don't have time for this so hiring someone is the only sensible option.

## NAP Placement
When it comes to local SEO, your NAP should be generating local citations. It's important that your NAP appears in any and all legitimate directories, especially local and industry related directories. Aim to get listings in your local Chamber of Commerce directory, Yelp, Citysearch.com, BBB, and many more.

Pay particular attention to getting listings in directories that have a local focus or a local section in order to strengthen your local SEO program. In addition, your company should be listed in any trade-specific directories. The more appropriate the directory in which you are listed, the more searchers will see you. The big traffic directories, like Google+, that get thousands of visitors a day, mean tons of exposure for your company to local customers.

## Directory Listing Information
Studies have shown that when consumers search directories for local listings, they would like to see the

following information within the listing, by percentage requested:

- Name – 67%
- Address – 67%
- Phone Number – 67%
- General Proximity to Location – 58%
- Hours of Operation – 58%
- Website – 55%
- Prices – 53%

This clearly demonstrates why it's so important to provide the directory with as much info as possible. Each additional citation gives your local SEO efforts a little help.

**Additional high-value data that boosts rankings:**
Whenever possible, add the following types of high-value data to enhance your listings:

- Logo
- Picture
- Video
- Lengthy Description
- Call to Action

**Some of the top local business directories:**

- Google My Business
- YP.com
- Yelp
- Local Chamber of Commerce directory
- Local Better Business Bureau directory
- Local.com
- Yahoo Local
- Angie's List

- MagicYellow.com
- Kudzu
- Dozens more…

Creating quality local listing data is time consuming. However, it is absolutely essential if a business wants to enhance its search results rankings. Every single directory should have as much data as possible, especially high value data as noted above.

Another primary goal of being listed in directories, in addition to live traffic seeing your listing, is to build citations, which we'll talk about next.

# CHAPTER 4

## HAVE ENOUGH CITATIONS?

A citation is a reference online to your NAP – your company name, address, and phone number, as well as your website URL. The big search engines consider your company's citations when they evaluate the online legitimacy and popularity of your business. Obviously the more citations you have, the higher your ranking and heightened value for your local SEO efforts. Citations do not have to be linked back to your company website for it to get credit (aka, boosts to your ranking).

Any mention of your company occurring anywhere on the Internet, with a link or without a link, is a citation. Here are some of the forms a citation can take:

- Company name
- Company name, address and phone number
- Company phone number
- Company URL
- Any combination of the above

As you can see, even the phone number itself can serve as a citation. A full citation should include the NAP – name, address and phone number. When a citation does not include all three, it is sometimes called a partial citation. Citations are a critical element in local search rankings. Studies have shown that citation elements make up one quarter of the top 20 overall ranking factors.

## Structured Citations
Most citations are found on company listings directory websites like Yelp, YP.com, etc. These are called "Structured Citations".

## Unstructured Citations
These are citations that can be found just about anywhere on the web, including in blogs, news websites, government websites, job sites, online press releases, etc. They are called "Unstructured Citations" and can also be valuable in helping your local ranking.

## The Quality of Your Citations Matters
Don't forget to keep citation quality in mind. Not all citations are created equal. Is the source of the citation a reputable, honorable source? After all, the quality of the citation is a huge local SEO ranking factor. It can sometimes be difficult to determine which citation sources are helpful and which are the other kind. You might want to consider getting professional help with your local SEO citation ranking efforts.

## Use Local Events to Gain Citations

Hosting local events, or even simply participating, can be a good way to build up your company name recognition both on and offline, and a great way to create citations and backlinks. Not to mention, events are a wonderful way to link your business to the local community.

In every community there are loads of events going on all the time. Each of these events presents golden opportunities to generate brand recognition for your company, along with citations and backlinks. Consider hosting workshops, 5k runs, charity events… the list is endless.

Participation in the following kinds of local events can help with link building and company brand recognition:

- Local sports teams
- Local concerts
- Business workshops
- Charity events
- Social awareness events (stop bullying, say no to drugs, etc.)
- Art events (gallery openings, etc.)
- Community improvement projects and events (fundraising for the new park, etc.)
- Storm damage cleanup (organizing and sponsoring cleanup after a storm, etc.)
- Contest type events (chili cook-offs, pie-baking contests, etc.)

- Holiday events (Halloween costume party, pumpkin carving party, etc.)

Opportunities abound to sponsor or participate in worthy local events and activities. As long as you are involved in legitimate, fun, interesting events that are held for solid, honorable reasons and not just to build ranking, you will end up with strong links and citations from good sources, like local newspapers, civic websites, and local business websites. Not to mention the positive impact your involvement in these events will have in the minds of your present and prospective local customers.

As long as you are involved in an appealing, worthwhile event that involves a legitimate organization, you will probably be accepted by the event listing websites. Many of these sites want you to fill out a basic form that consists of the title of the event, the event's 'what, when and where', a good description of the event, and a URL that directs people to additional information. This kind of listing will generate solid citations.

Sometimes it can be nearly impossible to get a link from a local or regional newspaper – even more so from local and regional TV stations and other important local sites. But by getting your event and NAP into their local events section, you are getting a citation from their domain. Remember, the quality of the citation is a huge local SEO ranking factor.

Next up, we'll take a look at how what your customers say about your business can help build your local online presence (or hurt it, if you don't handle this task correctly).

# CHAPTER 5

# WHAT ARE YOUR CUSTOMERS SAYING ABOUT YOU?

Customer reviews are one of the top ranking factors for local SEO, and for turning searchers into customers. Once people have found you in the search results pages, the absolute number one factor that gets them to click on your website and continue along the I'm-on-the-fast-track-to-customerhood path is your review record. If your company's Google reviews show an average of 4.5 stars and 20 customer reviews, you're in great shape. BUT, if your competitor has 50 reviews with an average of 5 stars, you have some work to do.

Key points to keep in mind about online reviews:
- They strongly affect how companies are ranked in Google's local search results.
- They strongly affect which search results websites get clicked by the searcher.
- They strongly affect customers' decisions about buying.

**Good Reviews Are Good for Business**

Positive online customer reviews offer strong social proof that your company is dependable and provides quality, trustworthy goods and services. Good reviews make it so customers are going to beat your front door down to do business with you.

The fact is, prospective customers will nearly always read your company's reviews, and compare them to your competitor's reviews. People consider reviews to be honest and unbiased, unlike how they may feel about what you say about yourself on your website or your Google+ Local page, which is part of your Google My Business account (more on that in Ch. 6). If they see that you have 8 reviews and all 8 are rated 5 stars with strong endorsement in the text of the review, it's a powerful indication that you can be trusted. The more they trust your company, the higher the chances that they'll make contact and purchase from you.

**Review Placement in Local Search Results Is Important**

Any positive online review is a good thing; however, only the reviews left in certain places affect how you rank with Google's local search results. The reviews you get on your Google+ Local page turn out to be the most important. Reviews on other respected sites, like Yelp, tend to have a bit less weight. Reviews of your company left on social media sites, blogs, forums, and less respected sites do not carry as much weight in Google's local search algorithms. That doesn't mean those reviews don't have value, though, because local customers may still see them and decide to buy from you.

It's important to remember that the content of people's reviews, and the information about the reviewer, can be viewed by anybody who looks at your Google+ Local page. By default, reviews are sorted by how useful they are, as determined by Google. They do this by checking out the reviewer, the length of the review, and the number of people who have clicked to indicate that the review was helpful.

### Google+ Local Customer Reviews

Reviews on your Google+ Local page are the most important, because Google thinks they can be trusted more than reviews left elsewhere on the web. And the Google+ reviews are the ones most searchers will see, because they're linked to the search results pages.

### How to get reviews:

How you get your reviews matters. If you go about getting them in ways that go against Google's best practices, you'll do more harm than good. If you try to buy positive reviews, you put yourself at risk for major trouble. Here are some safe ways to get reviews from your customers.

- Simply ask new and existing customers when they're in your business, make some phone calls, or send an email.
- Create a "Review Us" link on an obvious place on your website.

- Display banners and signs with a review URL at your place of business.
- Put the review URL on your sales receipts, business cards, and any other documents seen by your customers. Also include a small flyer with the review URL to go with things that you mail or give to customers.
- Ask customers to leave 2-3 sentences that specify the product or service work done. The text content within a customer review has a great deal of SEO value. For example: "These guys did a great job" is good, but "These are the best plumbers in Atlanta. They fixed our all of our kitchen and bathroom plumbing issues." – a more detailed review like this, with keywords, has 10x more local SEO value.

Never under any circumstances offer an incentive for a positive review. Google says you can ask people for reviews, but you are not permitted to pay or otherwise compensate someone for a review. You also have to careful how you ask for reviews, as many forms of solicitation are prohibited by reviews sites.

Don't assume that if you do a good job the reviews will come flowing in. They won't, no matter how much your customers love you. Most people are unfamiliar with leaving online reviews and won't do so unless they are asked. Of course, if they're upset with a company they might leave a negative review. Don't be afraid to ask for a good review, and make it easy for the customer to do so. Give out cards with simple instructions for leaving a review. If you don't ask, you won't get positive reviews. Simple as that.

Getting good reviews can involve lots of moving parts, but it's critical to the health of your business that you get them. There's a right way and a wrong way to go about getting them. It's especially important that the first few reviews are good ones, with a fair amount of text, as they will lead the ones that follow. You might decide this whole process is important enough to leave up to a local SEO professional to handle.

Next up, we'll take a look at one way Google is practically begging you to let them send more customers your way – and most small businesses don't take advantage of this great opportunity.

# CHAPTER 6

## GOOGLE MY BUSINESS

Google My Business (GMB) is a web page that Google provides for local businesses. It allows you to put your company info on Google +, Google Maps, Google Search and other Google features. Small businesses are encouraged to claim and optimize the listing potential of GMB. They can access their applications all in one location, and no longer need to make duplicate entries. They simply enter their information once and it will populate all Google products and services.

The idea is to bring together all the services Google offers to small businesses. In fact it's geared for local businesses, especially those small businesses that have yet to fully utilize all of the Google products and services that are available to them. In addition, Google My Business is now the default for current Google+ and Places and users.

Google My Business offers businesses a variety of services, including:

- **Update your info**
  Update business info on Google +, Maps, and Search all from one location. Businesses can update their information, including hours of operation, website URL, and other site details, contact information, etc. whenever they like. This information gets displayed in Google's Knowledge Graph, which is on the right of search page results.

- **More room on GMB**
  You can add photos, including product shots, pictures of your location, displays, employees, awards, and other business-related pictures.

- **Make connections**
  You can connect with customers directly by sharing news, events, and updates on what's happening using the Google+ page.

- **Reviews**
  Your customer reviews and stars appear on GMB. And you have the opportunity to reply to your reviews.

These and other Google My Business features allows the small business owner the ability to interact with their customers in new and unique ways, which ultimately gets reflected in their local search rankings.

Short and sweet, that wraps up Google My Business. Now, let's take a look at how you can use social media to boost your local online marketing.

# CHAPTER 7

## ARE YOU USING SOCIAL SIGNALS ?

Social signals are the shares, likes, votes, views, pins, etc. that people use on Twitter, Facebook, LinkedIn and other social media sites that are picked up by Google and the other big search engines.

When Google sees that your company is putting content out on YouTube, Facebook, Twitter, Instagram, and Pinterest, and that people are following and sharing that content, it has a huge impact on how they rank your business. Why? Because search engines view people's positive social signals as trusted and convincing endorsements that say something positive about your company.

These days, social signals mean more than just having a Facebook page. Now it's all about the activity and interaction. Some of these interactions include the following:

- Number of Facebook Pages likes, comments and shares
- Number of website URL like and shares

- Number of genuine comments on your blog posts
- Number of Twitter followers
- Number of Facebook fans
- Number of tweets that include your company name or URL
- Number of people that have you in their G+ circles
- And of course, number of Google+ shares and +1's
- Don't forget about LinkedIn, Pinterest & Instagram

There is a definite connection between social shares and search results page rankings. The more content is liked, posted, shared, and re-tweeted, the higher its value. The gulf between local SEO, social media and content marketing is closing quickly.

The takeaway here is that if your content is drawing people to your website from Twitter, Facebook, etc. then search engines will begin to see that your content has value and will gradually raise your rankings.

Social media marketing is a pretty involved task, and can quickly become time-consuming. However, it's an integral part of a Local SEO plan, and you can be sure your competitors are looking into it if they haven't started yet.

Next, we'll take a look at how you can publish your way to prominence in your local market.

# CHAPTER 8

# FRESH CONTENT PUTS YOUR BUSINESS IN THE LIMELIGHT

Making sure your website has a steady flow of fresh content is one of the best ways to boost your site's ranking on local search results pages. Why? It's not surprising that search engines favor websites that have a continual flow of fresh content. The thinking is that by adding new content you are drawing in new visitors. The more often you add content, the more new visitors you draw. The more new visitors, the more value the search engines place on your website and the better your ranking.

Google and the other big search engines understand that their users want to see content that is current, appropriate, and helpful. Websites that are updated regularly are far more likely to have relevant content than older sites. Simply put, using fresh content on your website will help it gain better ranking on search engine results pages. Search engines crawl websites more often as the content is updated or changed.

## What Kinds of Content Do You Need?

**New Web Pages** – This is the most obvious way to freshen the content of your website. But don't create new web pages just for the sake of trying to boost your rankings. If you discover gaps in the content on your pages or have new products or services, or new twists on existing products or services, then by all means, create new webpages to reflect this.

**Blog** – A blog is perhaps the best and most reliable way to create and maintain a steady stream of fresh content. Publishing engaging, informative blog posts at least once a week is best. Aim for blog posts that informative, relevant, and useful to the reader, rather than posts that are purely promotional. After you've created a solid foundation of blogs, consider turning them into an eBook you can give away on your website. Pick and choose the best blogs to create another piece of fresh content.

**Guest Blog Posts:** A great way to generate social signals and high quality backlinks is to get your content posted on other website that are related to, but not in competition with, your website. If you are an Atlanta plumber, submitting a post to an Atlanta foundation repair company is a great way for you to get exposure to their audience, and earn a backlink via and author attribution at the end of the guest post. You can also invite other local companies to post on your website. In both cases, the guest blogger and publishing site will promote the post in their social media channels, generating all sorts of great social signals. Strategic and targeted guest blog posting can create a cascade of win-wins for both parties. Just keep in mind, most of your blog content should be your own content, with maybe 20-30% max made up of guest blog posts.

**Community Activities Posts** – One way to increase your website popularity with visitors as well as search engines is to reference things happening within your local community. Local current activities will appeal to your website visitors and, in doing so, boost your ranking. For example, perhaps your company is hosting a local "5k Run for Breast Cancer Awareness". Your post would be a great place to mention the event, along with the fact that your company happens to be a sponsor.

**eBooks** – eBooks are a great way to re-purpose your blog content and FAQ's into a downloadable pdf eBook. Aside from special offers and promotions, an eBook may be one of the best call-to-action carrots you can offer a web visitor in exchange for his or her email address, so that you can build a targeted email marketing list.

**SlideShare** – SlideShare is an Internet based slide-show hosting service. Companies can upload files, either privately or publicly in various file formats. Interesting and fresh company data can be created and shared which will draw in visitors and boost rankings.

**Quizzes** – Quizzes are an often overlooked means of developing fresh content. A recent study of website content found that the typical website quiz is shared nearly 2000 times. Meaning a quiz you develop for your website has a great chance of generating significant interest. Clever quizzes are fun to take and draw big crowds. Big crowds mean higher rankings.

**Geo-Tagging** – Geo-tagging is the placement of geographical information metadata embedded into an object, like a photograph, or into larger elements, like websites. Geo-tagging your website is a useful means of boosting local SEO because you can include important data about your company that visitors can't see, but search engines can. This tactic can make your website more relevant to local searches that your prospective customers are performing.

With the explosion in the use of smartphones for local searching, it's not surprising that companies want to make it easy for search engines to connect their website to their physical address. By adding metatags, you can include location data, company information and rules that web-bots must follow.

Geo-tagging is the simplest and best way to have your website found by people searching within a certain geographic area for the products or services your company offers. In short, the tagging makes it far more likely that searchers will find your company's website in their local search results. Geo-tagging is not exactly rocket science. However, if you're unfamiliar with the process you might want to consider using a local SEO professional, because tagging incorrectly can cause problems for you.

Now that you have a fundamental understanding of the key elements affecting local SEO, it's time to take a look at some next steps you can take to put what you've learned to use.

# CHAPTER 9

## NEXT STEP

$Y$ou might be feeling slightly overwhelmed as you consider all the elements involved in creating Local SEO for your website. Remember that your Local SEO program does not need to be perfect, but it does need to be better than what your competitors are doing. If you're a small or mid-sized company, chances are your competition is, too. They may not be aware of local SEO and how it can help their business explode. But because you are aware (which is a huge advantage), you know what you need to do in order to boost your company's search results.

To avoid becoming overwhelmed – and still make steady progress – you may want to approach your Local SEO strategy as a long-term project. It's not a set of tasks that can be done just once, or done overnight. It's an ongoing project that will require patience and diligence as you work on it bit by bit. They don't call it "organic SEO" for nothing – search engines know what natural progress is versus gaming the system too hard or all at once.

If you follow just these basics, and do them effectively and consistently, we're sure that within a matter of months you'll be coming out ahead of your competition in local search results.

Trying to stay on top of all this is a difficult task for most small business owners. You've got your hands full running the day-to-day operations of your business. While it's important to have at least a rudimentary understanding of Local SEO, learning enough to actually do it is a time-consuming and never-ending task.

So, while you could try to handle all the tasks involved in boosting your local online presence in-house, it may not be the best use of your time. You might find that it makes more sense to outsource this task to a Local SEO consultant instead. Be sure to look for one who specializes in Local SEO, not just SEO. After all, you want to ensure the new prospects who visit your website are actually geographically close enough to become your customers.

We hope this guide to Local SEO has helped you understand more about what you need to do to help your local business compete for and win a steady stream of new customers. If you have questions, or would like to schedule a free consultation to assess how your local business could benefit from a stronger local online presence, we'd be happy to help.

Keep in mind that Marketing Guides is a full series of eBook guides just like this one that covers a wide array of digital marketing tactics such as Google AdWords, Facebook Advertising, Content Marketing, WordPress, Video Marketing, Social Media and more:

**http://ducttapepublishing.com/book-categories/marketing-guides/**

For professional help with your local SEO strategy, contact one of the authors and be sure to read Ray and Phil's bio pages below for special offers and freebies.

# ABOUT THE AUTHORS

**Ray L. Perry**
Chief Marketing Officer
MarketBlazer, Inc.
www.RayLPerry.com
www.MarketBlazer.com
www.NeedMarketing.com

**Ray L. Perry** is a marketing consultant, business advisor and author of *"Guide to Marketing your Business Online"* (2011), and co-author of *"Renewable Referrals"* (2014), *"The Small Business Owners Guide to Local Lead Generation"* (2015), and the soon to be released *"Do Leadership: A step-by-step Guide to Doing Thought Leadership"* (2015) and *"Avid Strategy: How Focus, Culture, and Commitment move your Small Business Marketing to the Next Level"* (2016).

Ray is also the co-author of the *"Marketing Guides for Small Business"* eBook series, which includes topics on Website Design, Local SEO, Content Marketing, Social Media, Google AdWords, and Reputation Management. Ray is a featured author on Duct Tape Publishing and a key contributor to the marketing training website NeedMarketing.com.

Ray is the Chief Marketing Officer with MarketBlazer, Inc., a technology based marketing agency specializing in small business lead generation, lead conversion, and customer engagement. MarketBlazer combines a proven 7 step marketing process and strong technology background with the latest in Internet, social media, and mobile marketing tactics to develop solid long-term inbound marketing strategies for clients. The MarketBlazer goal with marketing is simple and straight forward; help our clients' business thrive.

Ray is a Master Marketing Consultant certified by Duct Tape Marketing. Using the proven marketing strategies of Duct Tape Marketing, Ray helps clients develop marketing strategies to find prospects that have a need for their products and services, and convert these prospects into long-term customers that know, like, and trust his clients. Additionally, these new customers frequently refer Ray's clients' to other potential customers with the same need or problem.

Ray brings to the MarketBlazer team nearly three decades of leadership expertise in operations, sales, and marketing of technology products and services within start-up and high-growth entrepreneurial environments. With over 25 years of senior sales and marketing experience coupled with C level management experience, Ray understands the marketing process and its role in supporting the growth of small businesses. Ray's experiences as a technology sales and marketing executive and inbound marketing consultant merge to serve clients in an environment that is both creative and innovative. Ray knows that only sales results demonstrate marketing effectiveness. Having sat where you sit, Ray understands your challenges and concerns.

**Follow Ray L. Perry:**
www.twitter.com/raylperry
www.linkedin.com/in/raylperry
www.plus.google.com/+rayperry

Learn more about Ray's Books:
www.amazon.com/author/rayperry

## Special Offers from Ray:

### Free SEO Analysis

Do you realize how not having the right SEO on your small business website could be preventing your ideal customers from connecting with you? Make sure you are getting it right; your business success literally depends upon it! Fill out a simple form by following the link below to get a professional SEO analysis that will ensure you are doing it right and setting up your business for success online.

www.marketblazer.com/resources/seo-analysis/

**Phil Singleton**

Kansas City Web Design®
www.KCWebDesigner.com
Kansas City SEO®
www.KCSEOPro.com

Phil Singleton is a self-described 'SEO grunt' obsessed with tweaking websites for search engine optimization and functional performance. Phil is a Duct Tape Marketing Certified Consultant and has a B.S. In Finance from Fairfield University and an MBA from Thunderbird, The Graduate School of International Management in Phoenix, Arizona.

Phil is co-author author of the Amazon best-seller *The Small Business Owner's Guide To Local Lead Generation* (2015), **and author of the Amazon best-selling Kindle eBook** *How To Hire A Web Designer: And Not Get Burned By Another Agency* **(2015). Phil is also co-author of the upcoming book** *"Top Ten Marketing Tactics"* **(2016).**

A finance guy by training, Phil is laser-focused on ROI and passionate about helping companies generate more phone call leads, email inquiries and referral business. Small business marketing consulting, with a focus on web design and SEO, is just a means to this end. Phil believes that the Internet drives more purchase decisions than any other medium in history of capitalism, and as such has devoted the last fifteen years to working with companies of all sizes to significantly improve their search engine visibility. In addition to providing inbound marketing consulting services to companies in the Midwest and nationally, Phil provides SEO-friendly custom WordPress & Magento websites under the brand Kansas City Web Design® (www.kcwebdesigner.com) and online marketing and search engine optimization services under the brand Kansas City SEO® (**www.kcseopro.com**).

Phil is an active blogger and his content and blog posts have been featured on Duct Tape Marketing, Freshbooks.com, SEMRush.com, Ahrefs.com, AdvancedWebRanking.com & WebDesignerDepot.com and many local Kansas City and Midwest regional print publications and websites. Some highlights of Phil's unique career:

- Helped dozens of US startups and tech companies raise millions of dollars in strategic venture capital investment and cross-border licensing agreements in the Asia Pacific region.

- Ran the global retail and online sales divisions for a best-selling line of consumer software products.

- Started a software company in Asia, raising over $1M in venture capital funding, grew to profitability with 25 employees, then sold three years later. This experience in what got him into SEO and Internet marketing…in short by following the ROI trail to SEO.

- Is fluent in Mandarin Chinese

- Lived in Asia for over 10 years, primarily in Taipei, Taiwan, and briefly in Beijing, Shanghai & Hong Kong. Traveled extensively throughout the Asia-Pacific region on business.

- Lives in Overland Park, KS with wife Vivian and twin sons Ely & Ostyn.

**Follow Phil Singleton:**
https://twitter.com/kcwebsites
https://plus.google.com/+PhilSingleton
https://www.linkedin.com/in/seokansascity

<u>Learn More About Phil's Books</u>
http://www.amazon.com/author/philsingleton

## Special Offers from Phil:

### Free SEO Website Audit

Get a detailed SEO website on your website today. You will not only receive a detailed report on your website, but an electronic copy of the Amazon best-seller: *"How To Hire A Web Designer: And Not Get Burned By Another Agency."*

Get your free one-click SEO report here:
**http://websitereview.kcseopro.com**